Mindset Press: Conquering Your Thoughts with Confidence

Mindset Press:
Conquering Your Thoughts with Confidence

Carl Holt III

Editors – Mrs. Anita & Ms. Christine

Mindset Press Publishing
2017

First Printing: 2017

ISBN 978-1-387-04798-7

Mindset Press Publishing
450 Jackson St.
Columbus, Indiana 47201

www.mindsetpress.org

Ordering Information:
Special discounts are available on quantity purchases by corporations, associations, educators, and others. For details, contact the publisher at the above-listed address.

U.S. trade bookstores and wholesalers: Please contact Mindset Press Publications Tel: (812) 379-8729; or email carlholtiii@mindsetpress.org

Dedication

Dedication of this book goes to my family, friends, and to all of those whom I've met along the way that has given me encouraging words to help me grow. This book would not be so without the many lessons that I've learned from each one of you. So, I just want to say, Thank you.

I write this book with motivation and inspiration from my older sister, Lil' Ros and my dad. As for my sister and as she rejoices in Heaven, she continues to bless me with her drive and willingness to do whatever it takes to reach her goal. I've learned so much more about her when she passed away. As for my dad, he always told me to be strong no matter what I was going through. He continued to teach me and guide me, no matter how old I've gotten. He will forever be missed. We, their family and children, were blessed to have them the time we did. As we struggle through life, it is pertinent that we never give up. Never give up on the things that matter to us. Never give up on those things that make us better. Continue to strive for whatever you perceive to be great.

Contents

Acknowledgements

The accomplishment of this book goes to my family, friends, and to all of those who I've met along the way that has given me encouraging words to help me grow. This book would not be so without the many lessons that I've learned from each one of you. Throughout the years of many ups and downs, you all have helped me to grow and become the person that I am today. So, I just want to say, Thank you.

Preface

Hello there! During the writing of this book, I was faced with challenges and discouraging times, well – as we all are at times. This is what gave me more motivation to continue writing and pursue the opportunity to share what great things could be done by not letting negative thoughts ruin our lives. It is my hope and prayer that you choose to use the lessons given in the book to better you as an individual and help others grow. I've had to personally overcome mental struggles that have had me bound at times. Through love and support from others, I built my mental stability and learned to never forget that I am "Great"!

Introduction

Welcome to your new journey that you have just chosen to embark on! By reading this book, we can assume that you are in motion to start thinking and behaving in a more positive manner. In this book, you will find ways to challenge your mental behavior. By challenge I mean, thoughts on how you will continue to perceive your situation and how you are going to handle it. Are you going to wait until it's too late to make a change? Or, are you going to do something about your current way of thinking now? Let us hope it is the former of the two.

If you feel like you've been waiting far too long to make a change… congratulations on taking the first step. The topics in this book are pretty straight forward. Nothing is sugar coated. If you are serious about changing your thought habits, the time is now!

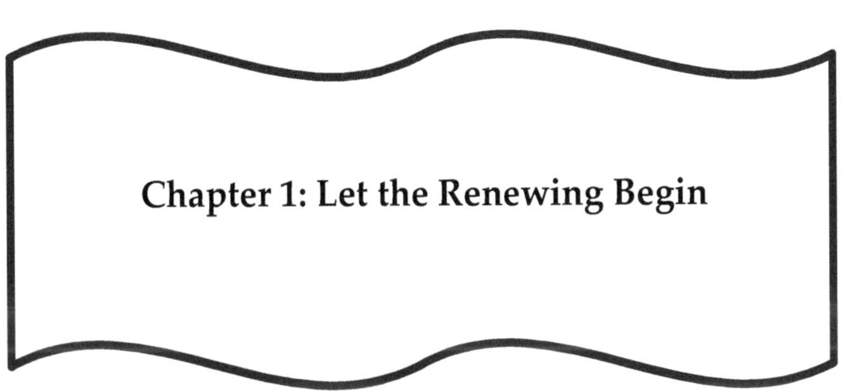

Chapter 1: Let the Renewing Begin

Do you ever wonder why some people are never satisfied with anything? Even when they are happy, it's hard for them to continue in that feeling of happiness. Probably the reason for this is that happiness is just a conditioned response to certain or series of circumstances. Meaning that just because something might excite them and they may feel "happy," it will not continue to reign throughout their life. Happiness comes from time to time, but it is not the driving force behind your mental well-being. Developing habits that will cause joy instead of happiness is what will get you to that lifetime of great feelings.

Happiness can be taken away from you easily, but joy – not so much. Your joy comes from finding what satisfies you personally. Once you find whatever that personal satisfaction is, your mindset will begin to change. Your actions will begin to display a whole new character. You will become transformed by the renewing of your mind. Doesn't that sound "great"? Imagine yourself having that feeling of happiness and it is lasting past your circumstances. That's what joy does for you. You have a higher chance of making it through tough situations whenever joy becomes a part of your everyday life. The need to seek happiness won't be as important to you anymore.

See, happiness fluctuates. One moment you could be riding the high horse and the next minute it could have you genuflect as if you're in the presence of dignitaries. Happiness is a good thing – it's just shouldn't be your main aim. It's only temporal. Think joy. Find your treasure. Alexander Zoltai said that using the conscious mind intently triggers the unconscious to supply its treasures. Once you begin to pinpoint areas in your life in which you know for sure will bring about joy, your unconscious mind will give you all the reasons as to why it brings you that joy. Your mind is full of many things that are ready to be released. Sometimes, all you need is the right precursor to help exonerate the enslaved trueness of yourself.

The purpose of this book is to help people to develop a successful mindset – a mindset in which Christ intended us to have. Successful as in changing the way we think. Not so much of attaining physical wealth, but more of mental wealth. Having a healthy mindset would skyrocket one's chances of doing something great. Once your mind is strong, you would be able to push through barriers and leap hurdles even with whatever it is, weighing you down.

Building on the building block of success means to overcome every obstacle one is faced with. Now, that isn't to say that you will never fail at times. Failing at something does not define who you are or where you are going. To become successful, one might have to fail multiple times. Let's define success. Success is whatever you need it to be; it varies from people to people. What does it mean to you? Don't rush your answer! Seriously, just ponder on what success really means to you. Think about it long and hard. To some, success might be getting that job promotion, a new vehicle, or even a bigger house perhaps!

Let me introduce a new way to help you define what success is. Allow success to simply mean "a new way of thinking." We become what we surround ourselves with. In order to induce success, we must look at what we are around; what we are doing. What are we taking in daily? Is it reading the Bible more often? Are we praying daily? What's in our earbuds? What's playing on our televisions? All of these variables and more play into how we define success. Mental note: if you are constantly hanging around someone who is always negative, how can you expect to become successful mentally? You will always have to battle within your mind in order to keep your thoughts at bay.

Changing how we think can alter our view of success. There was a time when I used to think to have success only meant being rich. Ha! Oh, was I ever wrong? There is a saying that goes, "more money, more problems". If this is the case, how can one think themselves to truly be successful if one of the implications of being rich, is to have more problems? Now, I'm not saying that a rich person isn't successful because they are. I am merely saying that no matter our circumstance, we can still consider ourselves successful.

You are successful, but only if you say so. You must believe that no matter your current circumstances, you are successful. Life might not seem as if it is going your way right now, but you can still believe that you are successful. You might have fallen short on many occasions; it doesn't matter; you can still think yourself to the top. Believe in yourself. Doubt happens, but don't let it overcome you. Besides, we are supposed to cast our cares on the Lord. Right?

Success is the positioning of your mind. Where is your mind at? Put it in a position to receive greatness, then sit back and watch beautiful things unfold. Our minds need to be reconfigured to believe that we are somebody special. I once watched a video on YouTube about a homeless man that someone had interviewed. He began to speak about how humiliating it is for him to stand on corners and beg for money (panhandling), and having to sleep outside on the streets. It was a sad interview, but I can honestly say that no matter what the man was going through, he was true to himself. He spoke of how people would walk past him and say, "Go get a job…you bum!" When speaking of this during the interview, the man quickly went into tears. His final words before the video ended were, "I am not a bum. I am a human being. Just because I am down on my luck, doesn't mean that I am not a human being." Even though the man was homeless, he still had the mindset that he was in fact, somebody. That is the same exact mindset that we must take in order to progress our positions and move pass everything that has ever held us back. Always know that you are "somebody."

No matter what people might say to you, always make a point to progress. See, people are more willing to tell someone what they "can't" do rather than tell them what they "can." Even if someone jokingly tells you that you will never make it or that you can't, those words still can affect the way you think. I once worked with a guy who asked me what I was going to school for. After I told him, he jokingly told me that he doesn't know why I'm taking classes, because all I will ever be is a *wheel slingin'* production worker. Oh, and ouch! The shot I took after hearing those words were devastating. To know the guy, one would just laugh it off because he was a nut. Nonetheless, those words pierced me. I was in the process of rebuilding my mental state. I was even co-owner of my first small business at that time too. Hearing those words nonetheless was still painful.

> *"A word fitly spoken is like apples of gold in settings of silver"*

Words at the right time can hinder a person's growth. That's why it is good to understand how to have a successful mentality. No one's opinion of you can become your reality.

Those are words from one of my favorite motivational speakers, Les Brown. What you think… influences your actions. That's why it is good to surround yourself with positive people. 'Yes, you can, type of people.' Proverbs 25:11 says, "A word fitly spoken is like apples of gold in settings of silver." Get rooted and grounded in positivity.

Success is contingent upon one's ability to overcome. Too many of us suffer from psychological denial. Sometimes we may go through tough situations and instead of tackling the problems head on, we tend to distort them until they are bearable. Bearable, but yet still bothered by the notion that the littlest reminder or trigger will put you back into the full negative feeling you've worked so hard at making it "just bearable.". It seems like a vicious cycle that will never end. So, when does it end? It ends with the renewal of your mind. Romans 12:2 tells us not to be conformed to this world. Do not allow this world to influence the way we think! Instead, be transformed by the renewing of our minds, because this is the will of God. He wants us to understand and accept what He wants for us.

I remember when I was reaching my breaking point in a previous work position. Going to work and not wanting to be there, caused me to not give it my all. Looking back, I can recall going to my supervisor one day and telling him that my machine was having too many problems and that I wasn't even motivated to be there. Therefore, I told him I was just going to leave. It was only two hours into the twelve-hour workday. I received a point for leaving, but I didn't care. Other times I would drag my feet getting to work and to my production line, which caused me to gain more points. When I did work, I hardly ever met my production quota. My quantity output that was severely lacking. The supervisor had talks with me because of my tardiness. I received a verbal warning because of me always coming to work late.

See, it wasn't always this way. I used to be motivated when I went to work, but my whole mindset changed and that caused the dip in my integrity. So, what changed since then? Let me tell you! I remember having a counseling session with one of the church counselors. She let me explain all that was going on. I told her how bad I hated my job. I even threw out how much better I was then that position because it didn't allow me to work to my full potential. Even though that was true, it still wasn't the reason for the change of my thinking. She let me go on and on and on. After I was finished venting on how bad everything was, she politely looked at me and said, "Well…it's not your job that's bothering you so much. It's not your job. It's you." Oh! The pain! The suffering! The agony of those piercing words! Those words hit me extremely hard. It felt as if I just got ran over by a train. That was my pride being crushed. Something much needed. In my mind, I was thinking that she clearly did not hear what I've just told her because if she had, she would have never said that. The truth was that she was right.

Her words stuck with me for a couple of weeks. After a while, I was fed up with her being right, so I decided to do something about it. I decided to change my thought process. I was determined to conquer my issues. I picked up a book entitled *"The Magic of Thinking Big."* This book helped me to reevaluate the way I perceived things. Shortly after, I was able to get my points back down. My quality stayed excellent and my production numbers raised beyond my quota. I was even asked if I ever considered becoming a supervisor on a couple of occasions. The next thing that happened was amazing. I applied for a position that came available, but I didn't get it. Since I was willing to pursue something greater due to my new mindset, a manager in another department heard about me. They wondered if I would be willing to apply for a position they had opened. I received that job with a raise and I was moved to a normal eight-hour shift. Even after that move, I'd received another promotion. Changing my mind helped tremendously.

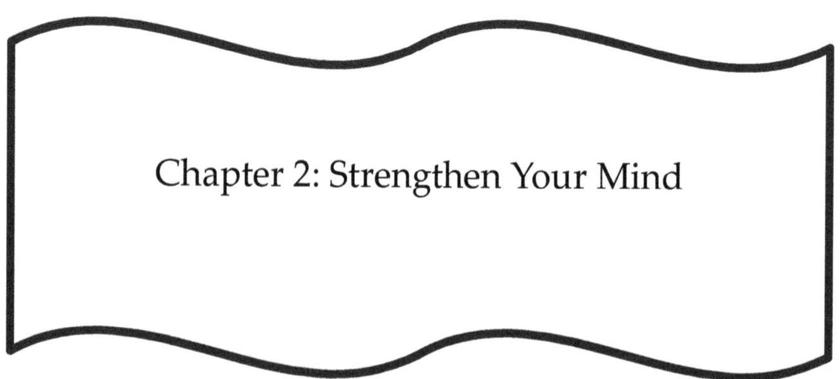

Chapter 2: Strengthen Your Mind

There is so much power in the mind. We can achieve amazing things if we just retrain our brains. Get rid of the negative thoughts and people that drag us down. Keep learning. Henry Ford once said "Anyone who stops learning is old, whether at 20 or 80. Anyone who keeps learning stays young. The greatest thing in life is to keep your mind young." Ironically, I was in a public restroom one day and while I was washing my hands, an older gentleman approached the sink and began to tell me that he was over his retirement age. He continued to tell me that he still works, but every day he is still learning. He told me to always ensure that I am learning because once I stop learning, I might as well give up my life.

Those were harsh words, but I totally understood what he was saying.

It always amazes me whenever I hear someone talk about receiving advanced degrees. We've probably all heard people mention that they have put in their time in school and that is enough for them. They say these things as if going back to school is the only way they can further their learning. This is far from the truth. Learning can come from reading books, listening to experts or people who understand a certain field, and from hands-on experiences. These types of learning require no money or little if any. It is good to learn something new every day. Doing so will stretch your brain and open your eyes to things that you've never thought possible. Joyce Russell said that "People who make learning a priority will often identify the numerous benefits of investing in continual learning." See, it is good to get rid of the thought that learning should be over once you finish school. It is never over really.

Don't wait until the "perfect time"

Determine what it is you want to do…and do it. Don't wait until the "perfect time." If you do so, that perfect time will probably never come. This isn't true for all people, but for those of us who say that we will wait, we might be using these words as an excuse for not doing those things that will progress us. Maybe it happens out of fear. Fear of the unknown. Fear of failure. Fear of the known. Or perhaps, it might just be the fear of progressing as mentioned earlier. An associate pastor and friend of mine once said in his message, *A Feast for Your Foe,* that once you get rid of that FEAR, FAITH IS RELEASED in your life! Put it in your mind that you will become whatever it is you want to become.

Once you determine your goal, go for it. Make the necessary plans, and then take the necessary steps. Feed yourself with what will help you to become what you want, or want to do. For instance, if you want to become a public speaker; listen to other speakers, go to seminars, watch videos, and write your own speeches and practice. Learn how to focus on the ones who display a passion for what they are speaking about.

Doing so will give you a better sense of the person who is speaking.

Get a true passion for what you want to do. Don't do it just because you felt like it one day. Invest the time, and sometimes the finances, in yourself. Let me turn this on myself for a second. These are the things that have proven true for me and every person who you may aspire to be like or rise above. In Ecclesiastes 1:9 it says that there is nothing new under the sun. This couldn't be any truer. Sometimes folks are too wrapped up in trying to reinvent the wheel when all they have to do is just roll with it the way plenty people have done before. There isn't anything wrong with tweaking a few things here and there, but there isn't a need to go get a patent for it.

Being observant to what is going on around you will help increase your level of awareness. No duh! Right. Think about it though. If you choose to observe others' behaviors, you will know what it is you need to do to reach the level you want or whomever it is you need to reach to help you gain your perspective goal. It is better to be proactive instead of reactive. Understanding that whatever your goals and desires are, they will include some form of help. A successful entrepreneur would not be able to reach their level of success without clients or customers. Even inventors need investors and even buyers. We all need each other one way or another.

There are some things that we need to do if we are ever going to be able to overcome the thoughts in our minds that tell us we are only going to be what we are now. One of those things is to have a plan. Plan out your goals! Plan out what your dreams are and make moves in order to achieve them. Once you've gotten down what it is you want to do, go and get it done. Do what you have your mind set on doing. Put in the work that will help ensure you will achieve your goals.

Sometimes you may have to push a little harder than others, but it's okay. It still must be done no matter what. If it's your goal, your dream, your desires; then you have to do whatever it takes to achieve them. After you've done your due diligence with how to go about your processes, check to make sure everything is aligned with your life. Don't throw away your family all because you have a dream and goal. Delegate yourself the time that is needed that will allow you the time to work on your goals. If you're married, keep going on dates with your spouse. Don't miss any of your child's games. Try to keep things at home as close as normal if possible. Take your tv watching hours and turn those into forward progression towards your goals. Now it's time to act on those things you were researching. Actively pursue your goals. Act also means that you should fix any errors in your steps that you may have noticed. If you have noticed, I just walked you through the (PDCA) process, which is Plan-Do-Check-Act.

Do you ever just sit and wonder about some people and think about what their lives are like or just wonder what is on their mind? I think we all do it from time to time. This could be a good thing and a bad thing, depending on your state of mind. Let me explain. During struggling times, you may look at someone who, from the outside, seems to have it all together, but they may not. Your first reaction will be that of envy. You would want your life to be like that at that moment or have their life even. This could be harmful. 'Be careful of what you wish for,' has been said many times for a reason. Just because they may look as if they have it all together doesn't mean they do. They could be going through something worse than you. They may only know how to hide it better.

You must focus on being the best you that you possibly can and continue to improve on your mental status. There are countless times in which people have come to me seeking advice and I was only able to give them blah advice. Deep down, I was sinking. My thought process had me in the mental state of uncertainty. I didn't know if I was able to achieve anything. Self-doubt ran rapidly through my mind. I could not believe I was ever going to achieve anything. When I say anything, I mean anything.

So, what did I do? Well, besides all of the access reading of other leadership books, watching leadership videos, and attending seminars; I did the most important thing first. I read God's Word and prayed. I prayed for a renewing of my mind. For strength and courage to do the things that He created me for. I prayed for peace in the midst of a raging mind. Once He did all of what I've asked, I was able to see things more clearly.

God began to show me visions of some things He had for me to do. I was renewed. Developing dreams and goals began to fill my mind. There was hope after all. Because of the change, I enrolled in school and now I have a couple of degrees, I have owned multiple businesses, I'm an author, and I'm a speaker.

I was talking to a homeless guy and he told me that he had plans. So, I asked him to tell me what his plans were. He started to tell me that his first goal was to marry the homeless girl that he was with. Then he planned on getting a car and a house. After he told me those exact words; he stopped talking. After a moment of awkward silence, I then asked him again – So what is your plan? He looked at me with a look that said, I just told you. So, I thought, hmm – maybe he's not understanding what I am asking him. I told him that he only told me what he wanted and not a plan. The next thing I had him to do was to explain to me how he was going to execute his "plan." He told me that he didn't know.

This is the problem, why do we have "plans" mapped out in our heads, but we can't figure out the first step. Far from his mind was getting a job so that he could purchase a car and a home. When I mentioned those things to him, he came up with all different types of excuses as to why him working – wouldn't work. I even told him about a mechanic that I met and how he used to be homeless. The ex-homeless man, whom we will call Jeff, told me how he became homeless. Then Jeff told me what he did to get himself back on his feet. Jeff mentioned that he decided to fill out job applications and he was persistent about working at a particular place. Jeff said that he would always call the manager, asking for a chance. The manager decided to open the opportunity for Jeff. An ex-homeless man now has a roof over his head with a little money to spare. Jeff thought himself to be better than his current circumstance and his actions proved to be true.

Chapter 3: Conquering Your Thoughts

Once you develop the right mindset, nothing can hold you down. I don't use the term "nothing" lightly either. It isn't good to have a plan without actions. A plan without actions is merely a dream. James 2: 14, 17-18 says, "What does it profit, my brethren, if someone says he has faith but does not have works?...Thus also faith by itself, if it does not have works, is dead. But someone will say, "You have faith, and I have works." Show me your faith without your works, and I will show you my faith by my works." The Bible states how we should utilize our faith, but also put effort behind what it is we believe God to do for us. Otherwise, we will not be able to grow if God just gave us everything we asked for while we laid around on the couch. It just doesn't work that way, and it shouldn't.

Let your heart bleed for those things that matter to you most. If you want something to change in your life, it is up to you to ensure that it changes. Michael Jackson said it best when he said that he was talking to the man in the mirror. Change comes from the inside and then it shows up on the outside. As your thoughts about yourself begin to change, so will your actions. Thoughts truly does influence actions. Did you not know that the wealthiest place in the world is your mind? It is so important to keep your commitment to your commitment and not stray away from those things that drive you.

"…you are special and unique"

Many motivational speakers have mentioned this quote: "It's not that we aim too high and miss, it's that we aim too low and hit." What is going on in your mind that is keeping you from being what you know you can be? I don't know you from Adam, but I trust and believe that you know you are somebody; you are special and unique; you are proud of whom you are; and all that you will someday be. If you weren't, you wouldn't be reading this book about changing your mindset right now. Either you are looking for a complete change, or you are looking to sustain your healthy mindset. Either way, it is good that you are taking the initiative to grow.

Who are you? Do you even know who you are? What are your thoughts when you are alone? Do you know what your purpose in life is? These are important questions that need to be answered. It takes time to get to where you are supposed to be. That's the problem with many people nowadays. Everyone wants to rush into everything and want things to happen quickly like slip on shoes. Growth is a process. Why do you think that human beings go through so many growth changes throughout their life cycle? It's a process and some things just take time to develop.

Understand this, things rarely happen overnight. For the most of us, we must endure what we must, for everything we obtain. Always remember though, God gives us all that we have and no hard work can add to it, as it is mentioned in Proverbs 10:22. It is our duty to do our part and keep our mind in the right place.

You cannot and I mean cannot please everyone. If you try to please everyone, you won't be able to be true to yourself. While pleasing others, you negate the fact that others make mistakes and there is no need to try to exemplify perfection when everyone is flawed. This indeed is a mental failure that a significant amount of people struggles with. It's the perception that they must do everything right in other's eyes. I had the chance to speak with a young girl, a freshman in high school, and she began to tell me about how she wants people to admire her. I am a firm believer that we should inspire others so they can be aspired by others. The young girl told me how she would cry if she failed at doing something because she always felt others were constantly watching her. She would cry as she felt like a huge let down when she didn't do things with perfection. Whenever she spoke, she would stutter a bit, is what she told me. By mentioning this, she used this as a reason as to why she would get so frustrated in front of people.

As I listened to her, my heart felt for her. No one should try to please people to the point of stumbling over their words. Confidence is key. I told her that I believe she needs to slow down and collect her words – even to do so before she speaks. Through her actions, I could see the frustration as she explained her situation. This posed a serious problem to her. Feeling the need to always please people leaves no room for self-actualization, which is to say the ability to recognize her talents and potentialities.

Therefore, I say to all, it's pertinent to find your potential and it should not be found in getting it from too many other people. If people are giving you compliments, that's great, but beware of false temptations. What I mean by this is simple. Have you ever heard someone tell you, "Hey, you should go into sales because you would make an excellent sales person" or "hey, why don't you become a lawyer because..., whatever reason they give you?" Hearing such things might make someone's ego swell, but the truth of the matter is that if your mindset isn't geared towards anything that you are hearing, you might want to think twice about your decisions. Don't just jump because others say so.

Apart from those people who try to motivate others into doing something they feel they should do, there are others who want to tell you otherwise. Whether this is true to you or not, we do live in a negative world where a lot of people don't want others to succeed them. My mom told me that misery loves company. You must stay clear of these types of individuals.

Someone once told me that you can't judge yourself by yourself, so don't be afraid of constructive criticism. With this, you must learn to distinguish between what is constructive and what is foul play. My pastor once said in his message, *"The Mark of the King,"* that you can never know what you're worth until you know who you are. Powerful, right? Indeed, it is. Understanding that you are a champion means much.

I have a friend who calls me champ. It feels great every time I hear it. At first, I thought he was calling me a champ due to me winning a championship belt in boxing. He calls me champ because of the many life and spiritual battles that have been fought and won through the grace of God. I want us all to do something similar to that. When you wake up in the morning and you make it to your bathroom mirror, look at it and tell yourself that you are great. Not great to be used as an adverb, but great as a noun. Great as in when someone mentions recording artist from the past or legendary athletes; in that sense. Know you are great! Don't wonder if you are, just believe that you are. If your mindset does not display this type of confidence within yourself, develop it. Keep telling yourself that you're great. You will experience some ups and downs, but who doesn't. Being great, being a champ, being a great champ exemplifies a person who is able to withstand what life throws at them. Even being knocked down doesn't define your greatness. Look at Michael Jordan, he did not win every game, but can you ever deny his legacy? You can, but you probably will be the only one ever doing so and you will be standing alone. Just saying.

One thing that gets me is how people can believe themselves to be worthless or minimal, but can't believe themselves to be great. Where is the logic in that? The calculating art doesn't seem to paint a pretty picture but does more to present indignities about the person. Mindsets that further their developmental progress with a mental state that induces indiscretion towards their own well-being, demonstrates the lack of self-worth. I know some of you have been surrounded by people who told you that you will never amount to anything, and you let those words become true in your life. Understandable. Sometimes we do become the product of our environment. That's what those words were supposed to do. Now, what about those of you who didn't have to worry about things like that, but you still allowed those negative thoughts in your head keep you in the same position as those who have had negative words spoken into their lives? When does it end?

I believe it ends with you making a choice to decide what you want.

Do you put a price on yourself, or do you feel as if you are so great, there is nothing that you can be compared to and no negotiating tactics could sway you to change the confidence that you have in yourself? Understand what I am saying here. There is a difference between having a huge ego and having confidence. Gain confidence in yourself and check your ego at the door.

Chapter 4: Outside Opinions & Influences

Often, we find ourselves surrounded by individuals who consistently complain about everything that is around them. This type of negative spirit can cause your positive mindset to shift downwards. You render ineffective results when you embed yourself around behavior such as this. You may even find yourself becoming a proprietor of the same behavior, whether it happens on purpose without you knowing. There is more to the whole complaining theorem though. Yes, being around individuals that complain about everything can cause your skin to crawl, but the purpose of this book isn't to change others mindsets – it's written to help assist in changing yours.

Now, let's look deeper into this. Say you are at work and all you hear are co-workers constantly complaining about the company, other employees, or their job in general. How long does it take before you find yourself putting your two cents in? You need to be honest with this one while recognizing that your little share in the complaining adds fuel to the fire. Once you have spoken something negative, it will stick with others for a long time if not forever. Know when to hold your tongue and when to speak. I might add, holding your tongue alone will not be good enough if your body language is conveying that you really want to lash out. I believe the reason that people complain so much is that they are trying to compensate for their own mishaps. Maybe they are not where they want to be, in regards to their positioning in life. Maybe personal problems are getting the best of them. There could be a million different variables that may contribute to the negativity they are spewing.

What if the world is made up of six billion of you and no one else? Would you enjoy that? Do you think you would like to be around people who act the way you do when you are having a stressful day? Probably not. By understanding this, you should be able to see that we all have an underlying reason as to why we act certain ways. You have yours and everybody else has theirs.

I recognize that we live in the real world and some people will never change, but you can. In situations like this, it is up to you to choose what you are going to do. You can choose to join in the conversations or you can choose to pull your coworkers to the side individually to talk with them. They might not receive you at first, or ever, but they might begin to watch what they are saying when you are around. Either way, it goes, you've just created a win-win situation for yourself. You can now continue to focus on keeping your mental fortitude strong and continuing bettering yourself without the distraction of negative influences. Your focus can't be on changing others. That is the problem with so many people. They are so worried about forming others into what is acceptable to them.

Look at this passage, Isaiah 64:8 says that we are clay and the Lord is our Potter. Since this is true, why are so many people trying to give the Lord a fifteen-minute restroom break and do His work for Him? You need not conform to this type of mindset. Know who your maker is and know that everyone else, well, isn't Him. You choose what you are going to think about and do; no matter what distractions are around you. At times, situations will call you to be stronger than your current circumstances. Will you rise to the occasion? Or will you shy away with less than perfect confidence in yourself? I'm hoping it's the former of the two and not the latter.

Your mindset does have everything to do with everything. Even when you are so "mind" conscious, it is still easy to get off track. The littlest things can cause you to not have such a strong mind all the time. Some time ago, I was having issues with my strength gains in the gym, so I looked for some advice. This guy began to tell me about gym psychology and how my mental state could really affect the way I performed in the gym. He told me that I could be stressed without even knowing it and it could have been that I was too focused on doing certain workouts, with a certain amount of reps, on certain days, which could have been what was killing me. I've never thought that I could be affected by that type of mentality in the gym. After all, I have done P90X workouts and I've heard Tony Horton talk about muscle confusion. Unconsciously, I didn't think that implied to me.

See, my mindset was too focused on achieving something and I did not give myself a chance to listen to my body. Having a strong mindset comes in different facets and it is important to understand how yours work. As I have grown, I can see the way my mind processes things because I am more aware of what my thoughts and actions are. Reacting isn't always the best things, but being proactive is. Train your mind enough so that it could mimic muscle memory. For instance, if someone is speaking negatively of you, train your mind to only speak good things about them. Do this even if they are in front of you. Another thing my mom used to tell me is to "kill with kindness." In Proverbs, it says it is like heaping hot coal on their heads. Do what you must do so that you are not tossed around like a rag doll with your thoughts.

Often, it's too easy to fall under the will of others. Even though you may have your own aspirations and dreams, others' opinions may seem to always trump yours. So – where do you go from here? It may be easy to disregard people from a different generation whenever they attempt to sway you to a decision. Well, what about your peers? It is pertinent that you do not allow yourself to become limited by the opinions of your peers. There are wonderful people in the world who would love to see you achieve your goals. Some of those same people may look to you for motivation, even if you don't realize it. These types of peers are feeding off of your positive flow so that they could continue to stay positive themselves. Peers such as these should be kept in your circle. Not necessarily in your inner circle, but in there somewhere. It's the others that you should be concerned with.

Peers of the opposite belief in you are not so eager to see you prosper. Trying to determine what to receive as positive and not so positive could be quite difficult at times. For instance, if someone told you that you shouldn't apply for a certain job that you might want badly; is this person giving you an opinion based on a positive peer perspective or a negative peer perspective? Understanding this scenario is a bit bland – how can you decide? You really can't, based on the information provided. More than likely, you will need more information to get a better read on how you should handle the situation.

Okay, once again, if someone told you that you should not apply for a certain job because they will be lonely if you quit your current position due to you both working well together; you should then know that your goals are not in their best interest. What you desire for yourself has now become secondary to them. Notice, they have put your wants for yourself behind their wants for you because it makes it easier on them. If ever you have been hit with a guilt trip, you can attest that it doesn't feel the best. You can't allow people's guilt trips to get in the way of your progress. Let's rewind a bit. Remember when I said that some people may look to you for motivation? Well, let's understand that if you are not empowered to grow, you will keep others down.

I want you to really get this. Others' success may be dependent upon your ability to show that no matter what – you will do what you set out to do. Get your mind set on doing – then do it. There's something that I always tell people when they tell me that they are "trying," and that is, "We don't try – we do!" Let that be true for you as well. Don't limit yourself to trying when you can exceed what you believe that you can't. When you do exceed, don't ever let anyone tell you that you won't be able to succeed in anything else either. Don't ever let anyone tell you not to do something just because they say so. No one with experience is ever at the mercy of another's argument. Always chalk the experience up as a win and continue to push forward.

"There would never be another you"

Know this is certain, if you don't step out against those negative peers, you'll find it hard to gain experience in anything. People become mummified from what others speak into their life. I come to tell you that I speak life into your dreams and aspirations. There would never be another you. Grip this, you are made uniquely you.

Chapter 5: Keep Moving Forward

Earlier I mentioned watching people and how you can learn from their experiences. You know what? Others are doing the same to you as well. One day I received a phone call from my children's elementary school. I missed the phone call, so I had to listen to the voicemail. The voicemail said that they had something for my wife and I and that we need to come pick it up soon. Well, I know that we just created some cardboard props for my daughter's play so I thought that we needed to pick up her items. When I went to the school, the nurse pulled me into the office and said that before she gives me what they wanted us to pick up, that they didn't want us to take offense to what they were about to give us. The school gave us a gift card with a balance of a large amount. They told me they admired all that we were doing to raise our niece and nephew. Of course, that meant a lot to my family, but looking into it deeper, I realized that people do really talk about you when you least expect it. Knowing this further assured me of the importance of first: taking care of business, and second: ensuring that no matter what life brings upon you, remain strong and keep moving forward.

You have the power to bless people with your tenacity to do well. You are not at fault when you fail. You're only at fault if you don't learn and grow from your failures. That doesn't mean that you can go and rob a store and say that you're not at fault; because you are. I'm talking about failing at certain areas in your life or trying new endeavors and they just don't stack up in real life as well as they have in your mind. That type of failure.

Do what you know to do and do it with everything that you have in you. Utilize your resources. If you believe you don't have any resources; look for things that have been done in the past. For whatever was written in the former days was written for our instruction, that through endurance and through the encouragement of the Scriptures we might have hope, Romans 15:4 ESV. Maneuver your way pass obstacles that may be blocking you. Pretend as if you're running back and your main job is getting pass defenders by utilizing what you see around you. For running backs, they see those small holes in the defense and they see the blocks their teammates are giving them. That is what you have to do. For everything that may come against you, there is a small hole that you need to be able to notice. Look for the kinks in the armor of your problems. No matter how strong and impenetrable they may seem, troubles are just obstacles that are in place to heighten your awareness for the next one. Do you get that? Sometimes, problems don't really go away – they just appear in another form sometime down the road. It's how you react that makes them appear to be something different.

Our reactions and proactive actions determine the true size of our problems. Back on the running back scenario; now what if the running back sees an opening and if he gets through it he'll score a touchdown, but he chooses not to go for it? He has now made his problem bigger by making it paralyze him for the moment. Your reactions cannot be such as this if you're planning on moving beyond your current position.

"Give yourself time to grow and develop into what you were meant to become"

Give yourself time to grow and develop into what you were meant to become. There are certain things that you must do that no one else should do for you. This is for the men – As a man, we have specific jobs that we must be held accountable for. As a family man, your main priority is your family. It is your job to ensure they are healthy. Healthy in all areas of life is what I'm talking about. Of course, it's good to ensure that your family is fed with good nutritious food, but it is more important to ensure your family is fed with good mental and spiritual food. You are the head of your home; therefore, you need to act like it. Protect your family from things that could be detrimental to their health in all forms; but for the sake of this book, we will stick with mental health. For your wife, keep her uplifted with positive affirmation and instill belief within her so that she knows that she is too "great." Make her feel like she's the best thing that her career has ever seen. She must understand that her thoughts are important to you. So, do your part to make that happen.

As for your children, with young maturing minds, it is your responsibility to start them out at a young age believing they can do whatever it is they put their mind to. Proclaim it. Speak boldly into their life. Tell them that they can supersede you in every area of their lives, but you must set the bar high for them; not by telling them, but by showing them. This means that you must do what you have to in order for them to perceive that what you say is true. Even if you have fallen short in multiple areas, you must still encourage them to be the best they can. Too many men are either absent as a parent or don't give their children the encouragement they need to grow.

We as men cannot live our lives vicariously through our sons or daughters. We might have wanted to be and do a lot of things as we were growing up, but things didn't shape out to be what we expected. Therefore, we put our children in sports and extracurricular activities that we never had the opportunity to get involved with and then we get mad at them if they don't perform to our expectations or if they simply don't enjoy the activity in general. This should be a huge disappointment to all men if you can relate. Develop yourself so that you do better. This isn't meant to be condemning, but an eye opener. One of the worst things for a child to say is that they don't want to be anything like their dad, because of poor decision making. It is your job to show your children what it means to be "great" – it's not good enough to just tell them. "Direct your children onto the right path, and when they are older, they will not leave it" Proverbs 22:6 NLT. Give your children something to admire. Work on projects with them. School projects, home projects, or even volunteer projects; it doesn't matter what kind they are, just make sure you are getting in that time with them. You'll be happy that you did. Show your children anything is possible.

If you say something is impossible, then your mind will make sure that it is exactly that. Are you one of those types of people who say "well, that's impossible" or something along those lines, whenever someone mentions something to you? Is it really impossible or is it just far beyond what your mind can comprehend? It's like when people criticize others' thoughts and ideas. People often criticize things they don't know or understand. I'm not talking about constructive criticism either. Are you one of those people who criticize others' thoughts and ideas? If so, why? Why do you believe that your opinions matter more than the next person? Just because you may have experienced over a certain area, doesn't give you the right to dismiss any one's opinion – especially in a negative way.

Now, if someone is talking nonsense that is one thing. If someone has a valid point to something, don't disrespect his/her thoughts because you don't agree. Having this type of behavior can be detrimental to the health of your environment. Your actions play a huge part in what you allow your mind to think. Let that simmer for a bit. How you choose to treat others is a reflection of your mindset. Everything begins in the mind, then it becomes the very substance that pumps through your heart vessels. Matthew 12:34 says…for out of the abundance of the heart, the mouth speaks. Whether you believe it or not, your negativity towards others is, well – you. You as in what you demonstrate yourself to others to be.

I find it crazy how so many people think that what they say is golden. Seriously now. My bishop says that it's goofy how some people are. Some people would just say, "well I just told them a thing or two." Who needs this type of negativity around them? I sure don't and neither should you. If you are this negative person – I ask you, why? What is the purpose for your disgust? You need to find what your underlying reasons as to why you act out in ways that make others cringe when you come around. If you haven't noticed yet, this book is to help you better your mindset; but it's not meant to do it in a way that sugar coats everything. Change is real and change isn't always a fun thing to endure. The benefits that you will reap are way better than you can imagine.

Remez Sasson has an article entitled, *"The Power of Positive Thinking"* and it says that positive thinking is a mental and emotional attitude that focuses on the bright side of life and expects positive results. Well, is your mindset congruent with Sasson's definition of positive thinking? It should be. When you read these questions that I'm asking, I want you to think about the questions before you continue reading. They are being asked for your benefit. I have a passion for seeing people succeed in everything that they do. That's why it is so important to me that people have the right mindset. It makes it that much easier to succeed. Even when you get knocked down, having the right mindset will encourage you to get up. Once you practice positive thinking enough, you will begin to see yourself and your surroundings in a different light.

Why do we worry about so many things that don't even matter? I was at work one day and some of my colleagues were talking about a little child who was shot and killed just before Christmas. The shooter was angry because the child's mother wasn't driving fast enough. Wow, really. Child dies during Christmas shopping due to road rage. How senseless how some people have made life. This is the type of things that show us that the whole world could use a mindset press make-over; and of course, a whole lot of JESUS!

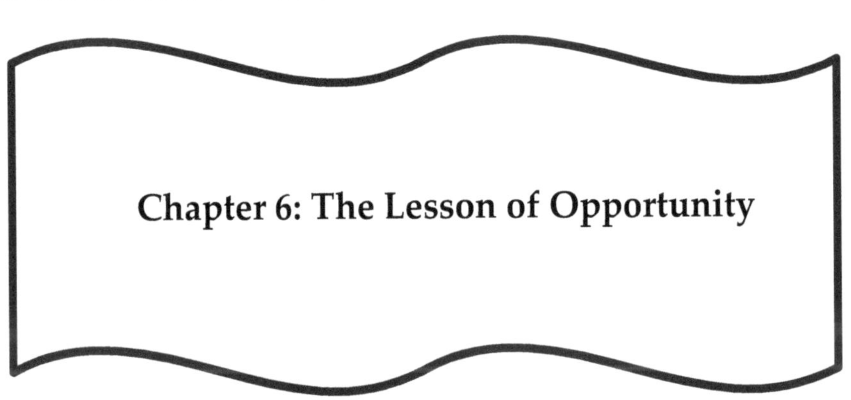

Chapter 6: The Lesson of Opportunity

Something should be said about when we choose to be determined about moving beyond situational factors. You will find throughout this book, I will reference homeless individuals often. My reasoning for this is because they intrigue me with their mindsets. So, here is another reference. In Chicago, I approached a stop light downtown around Christmas time. If you've ever been downtown Chicago, you will understand how crazy traffic is. Well, there was a homeless fellow in the middle of the streets – basically yelling for help at people in their cars who were stopped by the light. I remember making eye contact with the homeless man in which was almost two lanes away from me. He yelled at me, "Please, - please help me with anything!" He began to hobble across the lanes with desperation and determination – not bothered by other drivers frustrating looks and the cold weather; not the least bit. He saw me as a target and he took aim, then he did whatever it took for him to achieve his goal. We gave him the little cash that we had on us and he showed his gratitude, then he went on to the next person.

Now I don't know what he was going to do with the funds he raised and I didn't ask either. Luke 6:30 says to give to every man that asks of you and whoever takes away what is yours, do not demand it back. Besides this, Proverbs 28:27 says that; He that gives to the poor shall not lack: but he that hides his eyes shall have many a curse. We are instructed to give and rightfully we must do so. This isn't what prompts me to do so though. Helping others just feels good; it's this along with other reasons. I often wonder about certain things about their situation. What trips me up is where did the determination to do something after becoming homeless come from? Why wasn't the drive and desperation to succeed prevalent before they became homeless? Also, is their determination just enough to help them get food to eat and nothing more? I choose not to look at the people as individuals who are out on the street corners just because they don't want to work a real job – because you never know who is really in need and who isn't. It's assumed the true homeless people would be the ones who are sleeping outside when it's raining and cold. Nevertheless, what is the driving factor behind their determination?

I know that every situation is different and maybe becoming homeless is an eye opener, but I know that isn't always the case. Why is it at times that we wait until the last minute or when it's too late before we decide to make a change? Or how about this – why don't more of us who are in decent positions develop the mindset of the homeless man by choosing not to see our goals as far away when we're making moves? Things may seem to be astronomically impossible as we set more goals for ourselves. Don't let that thought deter you. Instead, choose to see it as a large target that is easier to hit than a small one. Pinpoint what you want to do and go after it. Lessons from the homeless – who would have thought!

Pass unsuccessful attempts can keep us from trying new things. Imagine if a child quits attempting to walk the first time they fell down. It's easy to imagine them not ever walking if they did. Logistical failure is when we try something and it just doesn't work out. Failure on a logistical level can expose what feels like an inadequate, child-like or vulnerable self, according to LPC and DCC Tina Gilbertson. Psychologydictionary.org says that fear of failure is a relatively normal and actually well documented persistent and irrational anxiety of failing to complete a certain task or meet a specific standard.

I do not want to focus on the negatives of fear right now, so let us look at it as a motivator. That word "FEAR" has many acronyms. I like "Favorable Events and Results" for this discussion. Going back to the child learning how to walk; isn't falling down for the child a favorable event? Some might say no because the child fell. Well, it's how you choose to look at it. The child falling didn't make it lose motivation. In fact, it did the opposite. Maybe not on that same day, but that child is motivated to walk and falling down just drives that child more. It is a process – just like everything else. Falling is favorable in this event. The end gain was the child received results by actually learning to walk. If you still don't believe me – what about when we have to discipline our children and we tap their hands when they're attempting to reach for something that we don't approve of? What happens? Eventually, they may learn the disciplinary reasoning and quit. Before that may happen, the child often attempts to reach for the object and sometimes repeatedly. They have determinant factors that drive them. As their cognitive minds develop, they merely react without thinking about the negative impact that reaching for an object might have on them.

As you make choices in life, allow yourself to be motivated by positive cognitive thought. Determine what you would love to gain in the end. Keep it in your forethought and never let it out of your sight. The minute it is out of your sight, you'll be more than likely to forget about it. It's like that old saying, "out of sight, out of mind." It can happen to anyone. If you find this happening to you – change it.

Issues shouldn't be bigger than what they are, but for the most part, they seem to find a way to be so. If you find something small happening in your circle arena and if you dwell on it, do you think that issue is going to manifest into something insurmountable, or if it will dwindle down to something not worth mentioning? The former of the two is more than likely to occur. Problematic circumstances dig deep into our thoughts for long periods of time – even if we try our best to discontinue the ongoing mental arguments of letting go of our self. When seeds of issues are allowed to grow into full blown melons, it becomes harder to flush them away down the stream of relinquishment; if you catch my drift with no pun attended. Once we make our problems bigger than what they are, what can we do to help our situation? When our problems are just too big for us to handle, our help is only one prayer away.

Zig Ziglar, a great motivational speaker, and author, mentioned that when we complain about the problems, the problems increase. When we look at the opportunities, the opportunities increase. When you choose to see your problems as opportunities instead of problematic circumstances that will deter you from moving full steam ahead, your motivation to do exceptional things will increase. Seeing everything as an opportunity will help to block out discouraging thoughts and it will help you increase your mental thoughts about yourself. Some opportunities will be challenging. It doesn't matter though. Don't you think you will feel more accomplished once you've put in the hard work and you reach your goal? Just think of the gratifying satisfaction you'll get from choosing to see your circumstances in a different light. You'll be amazed at how great you can make life.

Life doesn't always have to be one bad thing after another bad thing. Choose to make it one opportunity after another opportunity. An opportunist is a person who exploits circumstances to gain immediate advantage rather than being guided by consistent principles or plans. If a problem is considered a problem by you, then the plan that lies before you probably isn't good. Rather, choose to be an opportunist so that you may gain the upper hand in all circumstances.

Take your time and gather information. Gather information about yourself. We all think that we know ourselves, but, if you dig deep enough, you will find out things about yourself that you never knew. It may be that you've never allowed yourself to be in certain situations that would allow you to find this new-found information. Did you start digging through to that information yet? Good – I'm glad you have. Now it's time to grow. Developing new potentials and habits helps to keep your mind sharp. It keeps you thinking and productive. Notice I said productive and not busy. Too many people are busy but are not productive. You can be busy visiting acquaintances or playing video games, but are you being productive? The answer to that is no. You are not being productive at all, no matter how you swing it.

David Allen, a productivity consultant and author of *Getting Things Done,* said that "Your head is for having ideas, not holding them. Dumping everything out into a list can have a significant effect." Once you find out more about yourself, write it down. Meditate on your ideas. Recite them every day until you believe you could do well with them. Continue to develop these new ideas until you feel comfortable enough to speak to others about them. I'm not saying that you'll become a professional at everything you put your mind to. I'm saying that if you work hard at something, you would be able to explain how things function and know how to apply a basic knowledge to certain things. Sometimes we may need to give ourselves that extra boost of self-confidence.

"...discover a whole new you"

Have you ever had anyone say to you, "Hey, I didn't know you could do that"? Doesn't that make you feel good to know that someone has noticed a skill they never knew you had and they're excited about it? Why don't you allow yourself to have more of these moments? Excite and shock yourself sometime. Develop the mindset to continue pressing pass your norms and you'll begin to discover a whole new you. Besides, it's better to know a little about a lot of things, rather than to know a whole lot of nothing.

Chapter 7: Change Agent

Change is something that we all have heard someone tell us to do at some point in life. Maybe the person telling us that we needed to change was for the benefit of that person. Or maybe it was the downright truth. As mentioned earlier, change does start with you. No matter what is going on in your life; even if you might not have the power to change the situation, you could help it just by changing yourself. Think about this, say you went to work and all of your colleagues seemed as if they were bothered by every little thing that didn't make their job a little bit easier. You turned in your work, but you failed to use a spell checker or Grammarly, so you had a few mistakes. After you send your file down to the next person, your colleagues yell out loud "Oh no worry, of course, just let me fix it. That's what I always have to do anyway!" Oh, this makes you angry, even to the point that you boil inside. Even though you messed up a little bit, your colleague should never behave in that manner. Oh, and another thing, they don't always have to fix your mistakes. Even if they do, it isn't anything major. You'll show them the next time someone gets out of line with you. In fact, you'll make more mistakes and on purpose just to get on their nerves even more. No one has the right to treat you like that.

Now, since their attitude has caused you to react self-consciously in a negative manner, your day is completely hindered and your good mood is now gone. If this is you, it's time for change to occur. Changing how you react to a situation isn't guaranteed that the situation would not reoccur, but it does guarantee that you will feel better about yourself. The next time your colleague blurts out something negative, with your newfound change, your self-conscious thoughts will be positive. Things that used to get you upset will no longer have that effect on you. Changing requires some work and self-will. Perseverance is a part of the inward change. Once you are used to doing things and reacting in certain ways; changing that habit may take a little time, but it is possible.

Look at another example. Take a father who has a son of whom he will do anything for. If his son needs a new pair of shoes, the dad will go out of his way to ensure his son has them – no matter the cost. One day the boy said to his dad, "Hey dad, can you take me to the game in two weeks? My favorite basketball team is coming to town and I would really love to go to the game." The dad says to his son, "Well son, I don't think I'll have time to take you to the game. Even if I did find the time, your mom will just have a honey-do list for me to complete. Sorry son… maybe next time." The boy then looks at his dad and say, "But dad you always say that." What is the problem here? The problem is that even though the dad is always willing to purchase whatever material item his son wanted or needs, his son wanted something that money could not buy. He wanted time. In order for the boy to feel complete, the dad will have to change. The dad needs to understand what is really important. You must become a change agent for yourself.

Consider this. Isn't it great whenever you discover something, such as a new way of doing something? Or even when someone showed you a mapped-out plan on achieving a certain goal? The feeling of finding a new process that will make your life a whole lot easier is great! Do you remember that feeling? You see infomercials all the time with fitness gurus seemingly pushing you to do something. Something is always being sold. Whether it's supplements, exercise programs, exercise equipment, or even attire that makes you look slimmer. The thing is that some of these things might work. For the things that do, someone has figured out a better way to lose weight, so they decide to show others how the process is done.

This is what I have to say to you: achieve it, and then show someone else how. That is the purpose of self-help books and motivational speeches that you may hear from time to time. Actually, that is the way life should be. Why learn how to do something and hold it all in for yourself? It doesn't make sense. I'm not talking about an invention either, but even those patents have an expiration date. When you grow, you are supposed to help others do the same thing. Harrison Barnes said that "Every interaction you have with another person is a chance to make a difference in that person's life." This makes so much sense. Some people are present in others' lives only to plant seeds. Then the next person comes along and waters the seeds that were planted, and then the individual grows. We all are here to help each other. Look at how social media can portray an individual to be the greatest thing to ever happen to this world. Followers tend to mimic the behaviors of that social media star and dress themselves up to be like them.

"Carrying your past on your shoulders hinders your mobility to move forward"

Carrying your past on your shoulders hinders your mobility to move forward. If there are situations that have happened to you or if there are negative things that you've caused in your past; they need to be addressed sooner rather than later. Let's start with you being wronged by someone. I understand that some situations may be harder to address than others, but it still must be done. Understanding the importance of this is crucial. The underlying basis helps the renewal of your mind. Did you know that if you are carrying something around about your past with you, it affects the way you associate with certain people? Your relationships with your spouse, friends, other family members, and co-workers could be terribly hindered. Your co-workers not turning in their work on time bothers you so much, not because of what they did, but because of the bitterness that still soaks you up deep down inside. Arguing with your spouse and saying all of those horrible words aren't because they neglected to tell you they were working late or because the dishes weren't clean. These things are happening because there is something that's tearing you apart in the inside and you can't stand it. The crazy problem with this is that majority of us don't even know that we are carrying around anything. We believe that those things that have happened to us are just misfortunes of the past. We don't even know that we could still address those issues.

Addressing the issue doesn't always require you to contact the person or people who have wronged you. There was an article written by Nicolas Ellen about four principles to deal with your past. The first principle is "Seek to Overcome Past Desires in the Present." This principle explains that in order to accurately do God's will for our life, we must place our desires in their respective place. It goes on to say that our desires must fit our circumstances. We can't try to fit something into our life if it isn't the correct time for it to be there. Honestly, we don't even know if it will ever be there either. In other words, practicing delayed gratification will be suitable for this situation.

The second principle is "View God According to His Character and Not According to Your Past." Principle number two mentions that our view of God shapes our decisions concerning the problems that we may encounter. Basically, here we are dealing with the cries that say, "God, why did you let this happen?" Situations such as this, we now confuse who God is with who we want Him to be.

Principle three is "Confess Present Sin from Past Experiences." Repentance of present problems that we present to ourselves and just present sins in general, will begin to shape your overcoming of the past that haunts you. Lastly, principle four is, "Pursue the Future Prize in Christ." Simply put, Nicolas says, "In order to deal with the past, you must pursue the prize of being with and knowing Jesus Christ." If you are ever going to move pass those things that have held you back for some time, you will learn to know that life with Jesus will give you the strength you need to overcome.

Now, let us take a look at those things that you may have been at fault for in your past that have caused devastating and lifelong pain. Maybe that fault is just something that you think to be a failure. Or maybe that fault caused you to get a divorce. No matter what that "fault" may be, there is hope for you. Holding in pain from things that you may have done in the past can diminish your ability to grow. You are condemning yourself and when you do this, you can't make it to the point in life that you may have been seeking. Even if you reached that point with materialistic things, you won't be truly satisfied if you're condemning yourself.

Condemnation isn't from God. John 3:17 tells us Jesus did not come to condemn the world, but to save it. Condemnation tells you all about your faults and how you will never be able to recover from your circumstances. It tells you that you are not anything and you'll never be anything. Condemnation could come in different shapes and forms. It could come in the form of a condemning spouse who's constantly reminding you of your past. It could come in the form of ex-acquaintances always reminding you and others of your mistakes. It could even come in the form of yourself when staring in the mirror and the only thing you can see is your faults. You may even see a glimpse of something inside of you that scares you.

Conviction is a whole different ballgame. Conviction is the feeling that you need to apologize for your wrong. In repentance to God, and to those you have hurt. Having these types of emotions tells you "Hey you! Do the right thing."

That is why it's so important not to hold grudges against anyone including yourself. Conviction shows that you already know the answer to your problem. As harsh as it may seem; that problem is you. Now it's time to forgive yourself for your actions. They are done and over with, so quit reliving them by repenting and forgiving yourself.

Chapter 8: Importance of Self-Discipline

Ask yourself a question right now: "Self, are you disciplined enough to do what you need to do in order to succeed?" What answer did you give yourself? Self-discipline is the starting point for everything you want and desire. Do you want to be promoted at work? Do you want a successful marriage? Do you want to help others, and want to share your story? No matter what you want, it all starts with self-discipline. To be disciplined is to get up out of bed even when you don't feel like it. Being disciplined means staying up late, losing sleep to work on your goal. If your goal is to be a fitness guru, then you're going to have to be disciplined enough to get a healthy amount of sleep for your body. Discipline comes with a cost. It's the cost of losing out on some things that may seem important at the moment in order to gain something of importance forever.

Think about it: all of the "great" athletes and artists have had to be disciplined to achieve prestige and recognition. To stay aligned with the topic of this book, self-discipline is mental, the act of improving one's self. It's the counterpart of mental and physical success. It never ceases to amaze me how much our minds determine whether we're going to choose to wait for change or create it.

Why is the mind so powerful? How do our thoughts have so much impact on our physical selves? The gist of the mind's power can be explained by the "nocebo" effect, sometimes called the placebo's evil twin. The nocebo effect is often the cause of someone hearing bad news, particularly in the medical field. Doctors are in a tough boat when it comes to the "nocebo" effect, especially if they must tell a patient their medicine may have certain side effects or tell a patient they only have a certain amount of time left to live. The "nocebo" effect can cause a person to experience more severe side effects than they would have if the medical provider never mentioned them. This is the power of the mind. My Bishop once said that your future depends on your beliefs.

Well, then – do you believe you are disciplined enough to rise above any situation with self-determination to achieve your goals? Or, are you waiting for that drive to come to you, just hoping and pondering on what you would do if only you had your chance to shine? Just like the nocebo effect, your mind causes you to think worse of yourself if you don't choose to act on the things you want or know you could do. So many people live unfulfilled lives because they are sleeping their dreams instead of living them.

We all have dreams and aspirations, but few of us fully work towards them. Some of us work towards our dreams with full force but quit once we hit resistance. Some of us want that continual change in our lives to help better ourselves but quickly revert to bad habits at the least sign of difficulty. Sometimes that difficulty can take the form of the unsupportive people we surround ourselves with. More often, though, we quit working on ourselves or we quit being disciplined because of our *own* self-doubt. We don't even need someone telling us that we're not good enough, we're not strong enough, or we're never going to change. We put that on ourselves, single-handedly when discipline faces a challenge. All bets are off when that occurs. After all, who wants to feel like they're not progressing even though they're trying? Why try anything when all of the moves feel as though they add up to stagnation?

That's the type of mindset that keeps people from moving forward. People are all hype until it's time to perform. They freeze up and become paralyzed by thought. Standing out as someone "great" doesn't seem to have that same appeal to them anymore once faced with adversity. These overwhelming feelings result from an inability to recognize your level of discipline. Do you have discipline in the face of adversity? Do you have discipline when you want to relax and not work? Do you have discipline when your friends want to hang out, but you know you should be working towards your goals? Do you have discipline?

It's not okay to just get by with doing the minimum. It's wasn't okay in the past, and it's not okay now. If you want to change, do something about it; learn how to discipline your discipline. I believe that it's best to look at where you want to be—your goal—and hold yourself accountable. You might have heard someone say that you should find someone to hold you accountable to something, and although that is a great thing to do, that's not the same as discipline, to hold yourself accountable as if you are the only person you know.

Never give up on your dreams and never give up on yourself. You must continue to learn and continue to push forward. I believe our lives are meant to be much greater than what we allow them to be. You might get knocked down sometimes, but you have to get up. If you choose not to get up, then what happens? Life becomes that much harder; instead of getting back up and dusting yourself off and making moves, you're on the ground floundering and struggling. While you're down there, you're getting more cuts and bruises.

Look at it like this: if you're trying to reach a goal and someone else is trying to reach the same goal and you both fall, then should you choose to stay on the ground while the other person gets up, who do you think is going to succeed? Put it in your mind that you're not competing with yourself. You don't compete; instead, you supersede. You are superseding what you thought to be impossible.

No matter what happens in your life, continue to push forward. You are so much greater than what you think you are! Show up, and show results. Things are going to happen in your life that will make you want to give up. Things are going to happen to you that are not going to feel good. You're not going to want to go any further. As long as you live, there will always be something to go up against.

Exercising your self-discipline helps you to rebound, to react, to adjust, to change, and to examine situations objectively and recognize that they don't have the power to hold you down. Choose to continue to press forward. Make self-discipline second nature. Make it a reflex such that you create the tenacity within yourself to alter the way you handle situations and your thoughts on life. Discipline yourself to the point that you feel uncomfortable if you're not working towards your goals daily.

> *"People's failure to understand your actions is* indicative *of their failure to understand life"*

Some people may not understand why you're always thinking of new ideas. Some people may not understand why you choose to act on your dreams, no matter how risky. Keep in mind that other people's failure to understand your actions is indicative of their failure to understand life.

Don't be the puppet on the strings that everyone wants to hold. Be the puppet master of your own life. Containing self-discipline enables you to be just that – a controller of all good things, a recipient of the hard work you've done. The Bible tells us that we should reap what we have sown. When you're disciplined, you will always have a harvest. Amen!

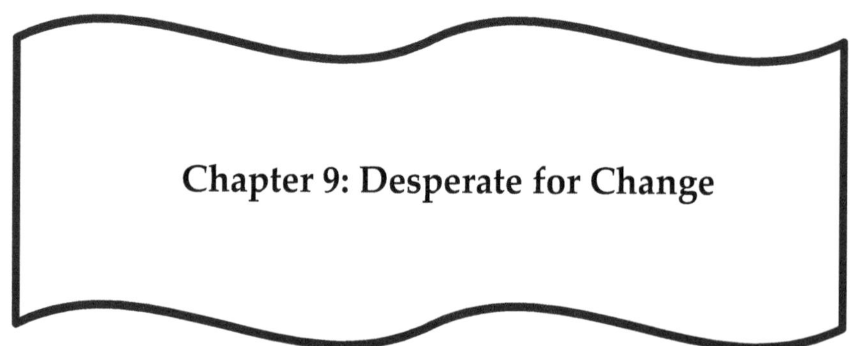

Chapter 9: Desperate for Change

We've all heard the saying "The struggle is real." At some point in our lives, we have all come across something that we just had to have. Let the desire to change be that something, that thing that you must have.

You know what? You're probably in a desperate situation right now. Perhaps you desperately need a vacation. What are you doing to ensure you get that vacation? Are you saving money so that you can travel, or are you just hoping and wishing the sky will rain a waterfall of dollar signs into your lap? If you're not sure you need to be desperate or not, then maybe we need to look at the word desperate.

The Latin root of the word desperate is *"desperatus,"* which means "to be despaired of." When a person is in despair, they sometimes become desperate to do something about their situation. It is a state of hopelessness that leads to rash behaviors. This topic ties into a later chapter about our capability to respond with either a fight or a flight response. Do we fight or run away from our desperation? I know you can see what the title of this chapter is, so let us dive into it.

Desperation strikes in the midst of trials. We all go through times when we are forced to do desperate things. Some of us learn how to pray in times of desperation. When you're broken and at your wits' end, you have no other choice but to do something radical! Years ago, I was stuck at a place in my life, and I really mean stuck. I was a full-time college student and I was working two jobs, both of which paid very little. I was bringing home $98 on average from one of the jobs after all the deductions. The second job was a night shift, and I was always watched on the security camera. After working the second job a few months, I was terminated for no reason at all. I mean life was hard. It's worth noting that I'm married with four children as well. So, I was quickly losing the sense of being a real man. I chose to start taking out school loans to help offset things my family needed. I racked up debt quickly. After a while, I put in my notice to leave my other job that brought home the $98 checks.

My brother had a dream of owning his own cleaning business, and with some of that money from the debt I accrued I chose to help him get started with his dream. He kicked me some accounts and I was able to earn more money working that job than I was with the two previous jobs put together. To top it all off, I was working much better hours, and I was able to focus on my hobby: recording music. I began to record artists from my in-home studio and earn some extra cash. Desperate for a change, I helped someone else out and it worked in my favor in the long run.

Sometimes, in order to progress, you might have to put someone else's needs and dreams ahead of your own. You never know how it will turn out in your favor. Although it took years for me to get to that point of desperation, I still made the choice to do something about it. I've met some great recording artists along the way, and my attorney works at one of the cleaning accounts I used to have. God works in ways that may seem to be mysterious. He works in ways that are far beyond our comprehension.

I've struggled for the longest time, and occasionally clouds of self-doubt still loom overhead. When they do, I look at how far I've come, how many people my life has touched, and how many more lives I want to reach. It never stops with me. There is always more, and there will always be more people who will need help.

For instance, those struggling with addiction need help and support. Let me take this moment to talk to those of you who are struggling with addiction. It doesn't matter what kind of addiction because no addiction is better or worse than another. Addiction is life changing for the addict and for the addict's families, friends, and victims. If you're struggling with something, this chapter is for you.

Let me put it out there that I have struggled with addiction in the past, and my dad struggled with drug addiction. It can ruin your life. Growing up with a dad who struggled with drugs was difficult. My siblings and I could never get things we needed, let alone the things we may have wanted. My second oldest sister struggled for the longest time because she believed that she was never able to live to her full potential due to the drug use in our family.

I understand that change only happens when a person is willing to take action, and when a person is desperate enough to make adjustments. I know that addiction is a real and true struggle. Addiction is a death grip on a person's life that is not easily loosened.

Let's take a look at the science behind what can aid in addiction. Dopamine is a neurotransmitter that helps control the brain's reward and pleasure centers. Dopamine also helps regulate movement and emotional responses, and it enables us to not only see rewards but to take action to move toward them as well. People with low dopamine activity may be more prone to addiction. The presence of a certain kind of dopamine receptor is also associated with sensation-seeking people, more commonly known as "risk takers" (Psychology Today).

As you can see, it's understood that having an addiction plays a major role in a person's mental well-being. There is no perfect treatment for individuals who are struggling. It is my hope that you, or someone you know, will choose to seek out the necessary help that will lead to a promising future. Show that you are desperate to make some changes. Be desperate enough to do whatever it takes to ensure your choices are healthy. I believe in you, and I believe you will show desperation to change.

"Open an opportunity for yourself"

When you get desperate enough to appreciate that a change is needed, you should create change for your life. Open an opportunity for yourself. I don't know what that would mean for you and your circumstances, but I know that there is a wealth of opportunity just waiting for you to grab it.

I had to create an opportunity for myself. Either I was stepping out on faith or being a nuisance, and I was determined to progress. Seriously, I've contacted people over and over again until they felt like they had to say yes to me. Networking on social sites proves to be very effective! Contacting people from around the world to help me develop this book was something that had to be done. I was determined enough to make sure what I wanted to accomplish was going to happen. I reached out, and some people reciprocated.

That's the pattern. You have to do the work, and the benefits of your work will do the rest. I will be completely honest with you: it's not going to be easy. Some things may be easier than others, but expect to grind your way through. I had a conversation with my son about being desperate. I told him that if he wanted to succeed—in any area of his life, but particularly in football, which was his sport at the time—that he had to be desperate and determined enough to get up on his own and train. I told him to do pushups on his own and not wait until I told him to do so. If you're going to grow in any way, whether physically, mentally, or spiritually, you must be desperate enough to make it happen. It's time to start taking initiative. Don't rest on yourself. Why are you sleeping on things that need to be done? I know so many people who need and want countless things to happen for them, but they choose not to go after any of them. When I speak to them about it, they always say something along the lines of them not being motivated enough to do so. Or they say the desire to get what they want isn't there, that they are content with the status quo. That's all fine, but, in reality, they still want to do other things. Perhaps the main issue isn't motivation. After all, if you can't find motivation enough around you, then it could be a good idea to check your surroundings. Maybe the main issue is a lack of knowledge.

You know the saying, that knowledge is power? It's also been said that knowledge alone isn't the real power, but that applied knowledge is power. Therefore, it does no good for you to read this book and learn that you could make a change if you're not going to go out and make a change. The title of this book is *Mindset Press* for a reason. You must press through the way your mentality sometimes weighs on you. Press through those times of denial. Even press through the voices that you hear when no one else is around. Only then will you see the direct results of your determination to move beyond your desperate times.

Chapter 10: Breathe Life & Exhale Its Problems

A 20th-century poet by the name of Robert Frost wrote in his poem *"A Servant to Servants"* that the best way out is always through. Everyone is equipped with either the fight or flight response, the willingness to endure and grow or the "I'm getting the heck out of here" response. Whatever you call it, you have one of these traits. These types of responses describe how a person reacts to an actual threat or perceived threat to the environment.

"Change inspires change"

American physiologist Walter Cannon termed the fight or flight response and noted that inside the body, a chain of rapidly occurring reactions activates the body's resources to deal with threatening circumstances. Hmm. Does it make sense to you now? Well it should, because like I said, it's in all of us. Going through tough times doesn't always have to be an "oh woe is me" or a form of self-commiseration. The problem is here – in existence – and probably not going anywhere. Glory in your tribulations. When you do – you grow. When you grow – others see your new height, and it makes them want to grow. This is true whether they admit it or not. Change inspires change. The inspiration that others may get might not always be positive – if you catch my drift. It doesn't matter though. What matters is you looking at your situation and telling it, "Situation – you don't faze me, not one bit. I might be shaken for only a minute, but once I regain my composure – you better look out!" Speak that with authority. Say it like you mean it. If you don't and you continue to carry it around, your problems will get the best of you and weigh you down to the point of sciatica. As you are taking in all that life have to offer, breathe it in and exhale its problems. Don't be discouraged, my good friend. Instead, choose to see your circumstances as a target. Get your bow and take aim.

There's a story about three manufacturing workers, David Kelsey, Tyron Johnson, and Melvin McKowski. David was that worker who was always at work – on time, and one who did a good job. Tyron, on the other hand, was a goofball who would take a mile if you've given him an inch. Tyron just did enough not to get fired. Melvin worked harder than both David and Tyron, but Melvin had a huge flaw. Yes, he worked harder than the other two, but he would talk negatively about them in order to make himself look better. One day, David felt the pressure from the other two, but in different ways. With Tyron, David had to carry the weight because Tyron was in one of his "I don't feel like doing anything today" moods. With all of this extra work, David overheard Melvin talking bad about him. David was quickly frustrated – even so to the point of his blood pressure rising. His hands began to sweat as tools began to slip from his palms. David has never said anything negative about any of his co-workers, no matter what he thought of them. David had suspicions about Melvin being a backbiter, but he'd never heard it for himself.

See, David was raised in a good Christian household and his parents taught him excellent family values. He was always taught that if he treated people good, then good will come to him. In his current situation, he couldn't see the truth in that. All of the hard work that David prides himself in, he feels amounts to nothing. Oh, but David knew of a great God, and he understood that his circumstances don't have to continue to be the story of his life. Before reacting in a manner that would worsen his situation, David looked to the heavens and prayed a simple prayer:

> Father, you see where I am right now and in my current circumstance. I believe that your holy word is true, and although I have faults and failures, I choose to believe you are hearing my prayer right now. Father, your word tells me that you are a rewarder of those who diligently seek you. So here I am. Humbling myself before

your throne – and I ask you, to first cleanse me with your Holy Spirit and forgive me if I've wronged my co-workers. Secondly, let your light shine through me and turn my situation around here at work. As I continue to seek your will – upgrade my life so that I may fulfill your purpose. Amen.

As the prayer began to cease, David found himself feeling lifted. David felt the frustration leave him and his thoughts became clearer. He understood that every time isn't going to be a benefit to him – and he may have to deal with trying times. Through David's effort of wanting to not stay bound mentally, he chose to exhale all his problems through prayer. David found a way to generate positive energy. He was able to find what supply would suit him better. Prayer worked for him, but for others maybe a little bit of peace and quiet might suffice for the time being.

Let's look at it this way, using electricity and how it can be conducted. Electricity has multiple ways in which it could be produced. One of those ways is through the use of magnets. If you have a coil of copper wire and a magnet is moved quickly in the midst of it; electricity is created through the movement of electrons. Life can be this way to us at times. At times, life may have us wrapped up in wearies and it may be hard to move. Therefore, we become stagnant. We either choose not to move or we're slow to move. Our energy may be zapped and the feeling of no hope covers our thoughts like a blanket of snow. Just as magnets conduct energy through being bound; we must do the same thing.

Take the position life has thrown at you, and make it work to your benefit. Use your situation as motivation to create momentum to eject yourself into another dimension of "this is your time" type of faith. There's no need to hold on to the "what is" and look towards the "what will be" once the energy you stir up produce so many electrons, the accelerated force from your rapid mental movement will cause you to glow so bright that GE will have to create a whole new wattage for you. Life gets hard. You'll have to admit that. It's not always good for most of us and some of us have it a little bit rougher than some. We may not understand the meaning of all of this, but it's not necessary either.

Martin Luther King stated in his *"I Have a Dream"* speech that he had a dream that one day his children would not be judged by the color of their skin, but by the contents of their character. What is said about your character? What are people saying about how you carry yourself? What do you stand for – that no matter the circumstance, you remain firmly grounded in your position? According to Merriam-Webster, character is the main or essential nature especially as strongly marked and serving to distinguish. Dictionary.com records character as our moral or ethical quality.

What sets you apart from all others around you? Find what that is, hone in on it, and water it until it grows to its fullest potential. What is it that you do, that it causes change to your environment? When you walk down the halls of work or school, what do you believe the thoughts of you are? Does your character carry a weight that demonstrates you are a person of integrity, or does it tell others that you don't care much about them or their thoughts? As Les Brown put it; thoughts influence actions. How you perceive others will show in your actions. How you perceive yourself shows in your actions. You can't possibly think that the negativity you feel for your coworkers is not being displayed outwardly. Think about it. The same goes for what you believe about yourself. If you think you're a loser, chances are you are going to be a loser – if you are not already one. If thinking downwardly on yourself breathes negative results, what makes you believe thinking positively about yourself would not yield great outcomes of achievement? Once again, think about it.

Your character yields whatever results it entertains. Define yourself. Look at it like this, does your character examples these statements:

> A person built on the great quality of character won't exploit others' weaknesses, but rather offer a helpful word in a time of despair. A person built on the great quality of character will tell you to do well, even when they are faced with difficult times. A person built on the great quality of character looks to right their wrongs

because the thought of not is too much to bear. A person built on the great quality of character will pray for you, even in the midst of their own uncertainty. A person built on the great quality of character trusts in the Lord and leans not on his/her own understanding. A person built on the great quality of character learns from life and teaches from experience. A person built on the great quality of character knows no stranger, but watches who he lets in his house; for he knows that his great character could be seen as a sign of weakness. Oh, but little does the foe know, - a person built on the great quality of character is one of the strongest types of people in the world, with mental fortitude and strength that matches the God-given physical strength of Samson.

Now tell me, where does your character reside? As you've read this book, I hope that you could understand the power that your thoughts possess. Not every change can happen overnight. I do believe that the most valuable change is a process and it takes time to get where you need to be. Take care of yourself, your family, and your friends. Continue to grow positively and in faith. God Bless.

God Bless!

I Am Somebody

I am somebody
I am special and unique
I am proud of who I am
And all that I will someday be
I have made many mistakes
But by those, I will not be defined
As I continue to progress
Positive possibilities are realized
I inspire to be great
No matter my circumstance
Creating change is a must
My life, I will enhance
So when you see me, please know
Through my faults, I have grown
And through the whole process,
Dedication is what I've shown
Life will never hold me back,
From all that I'm supposed to be
Just like I've mentioned before,
I am somebody, special and unique

How About Doing Me A Favor?

If you enjoyed reading *Mindset Press,* please leave a review on Amazon. Even a small review will do wonders for me. Your help serves a bigger purpose. It helps to prompt others to purchase this book so they can learn the importance of mindset change.

If someone you know could use an uplifting of the mind, please give him or her a copy of this book. Rather you gift the book from my website or any other, it makes no difference to me.

If you'd like to order copies of this book for corporate use, school, or a book club, please go to mindsetpress.org

Keep your mind strong. Press on!

Thank You!

Notes

"A word fitly spoken is like apples of gold in settings of silver." Proverbs 25:11

- This scripture tells us of how important it is for us to watch the words that we speak. No matter what we think, there is a time and a place to speak. Even if you're one hundred percent right – speaking at the wrong time could make you one hundred percent wrong.

Don't wait until the "perfect time."

- Often, we wait to capitalize on an opportunity instead of just going for it. The problem with that is this, the opportunity may never come to us. Therefore, why wait for a perfect time instead of creating the perfect time. Sometimes we must make moves on our own.

You are special and unique.

- No matter what life brings to the table for you, you must remember that you are special and unique in every way. You are created for a purpose. Now, go and find that purpose and execute it.

There would never be another you.

- There are billions of people in the world, but there would never be another you. Hold on to that fact and show others that you mean business. Continue to progress in every endeavor and stay strong.

Give yourself time to grow and develop into what you were meant to become.

- Progression takes time. Your physical growth doesn't happen overnight, so why believe that your mental growth will? Take your time and learn all you must…then you notice your mental growth sky rocketing!

Develop the mindset to continue pressing pass your norms and you'll begin to discover a whole new you.

- You can take these words at face value. They are self-explanatory and to the point. Keep developing yourself until you reached the highest of the highest.

Carrying your past on your shoulders hinders your mobility to move forward.

- Let go of the pain and shame that keep you bound. Forget about what people say about you and continue to march forward to the beat of your own drum!

Change inspires change.

- You are being watched even if you don't like or expect it. If you choose to change, people notice. If you choose not to, people still notice. So many people may desire to be in the position you're in. Hold it well and inspire them to succeed and grow.

About the Author

Carl Holt III is an entrepreneur, owner and operator of several

businesses, and an author with a unique and rare talent. He is also a native of Gary IN, a husband, a father of four, and an adoptive parent of his niece and nephew. Coupled with his exceptional writing skills, Carl has a Bachelor's in Criminal Justice and a Master's in Management. Growing up, Carl's life was not a walk in the park as he had to struggle. Despite this, his hard work, dedication, and determination helped him learn that life does not always have to be a struggle. For this, he has continually progressed in every area of his life and has continued to grow and try out new things! Carl is an outgoing and fun individual who continues to motivate his children to always give their best in all they do. He aspires to do well and hopes to inspire others to do the same.

Write Your Thoughts Here!

www.ingramcontent.com/pod-product-compliance
Ingram Content Group UK Ltd.
Pitfield, Milton Keynes, MK11 3LW, UK
UKHW020241250726
13967UKWH00001B/488

9 781387 047987